The Republic of the Husband

Lucy Tunstall was born in London in 1969. A selection of her poems appeared in the anthology *New Poetries V* (Carcanet, 2011). She has an MA from the University of Bristol in English Poetry and its Contexts from the Renaissance to the Present Day, and is currently completing a PhD at the University of Exeter.

LUCY TUNSTALL

The Republic of the Husband

CARCANET

Acknowledgements

'Remembering the Children of First Marriages' was first published in the *Paris Review Daily*. Other poems in this book were first published in *PN Review* and in *New Poetries V* (Carcanet, 2011).

First published in Great Britain in 2014 by
Carcanet Press Limited
Alliance House
Cross Street
Manchester M2 7AQ

www.carcanet.co.uk

A CIP catalogue record for this book is available from the British Library

ISBN 978 1 84777 256 5

The publisher acknowledges financial assistance from Arts Council England

Typeset by XL Publishing Services, Exmouth
Printed and bound in England by SRP Ltd, Exeter

For my sister, Catherine

Contents

I
The Children of First Marriages

II
The Republic of the Husband

III
Land- and Seascapes

I

The Children of First Marriages

Remembering the Children of First Marriages

Oh remember the children of first marriages
For they are silent and awkward in their comings and their goings;
For the seal of the misbegotten is upon them;
For they walk in apology and dis-ease;
For their star is sunk;
For their fathers' brows are knitted against them;
For they bristle and snarl.
All you light-limbed amblers in the sun,
Remember the grovellers in the dark;
The scene-shifters, the biders, the loners.

Traction

My mother's grandmother wore black for years and years,
lived among laurel and yew in a lodge at the big house,
where Charlie, her unmarried brother, slept under the eaves
on a sort of ledge. No-one knows why it was Charlie
took off, slow as slow, with nothing for the journey
but an onion and a piece of sharp cheese, to pilot his
traction engine, by a seam of moonlight on the river,
as far east as Isleworth, by way of Maidenhead and Old Windsor.

Aunt Jane and the Scholar

In 1956, or thereabouts,
Aunt Jane fell in love with a beautiful
scholar from the subcontinent.

Her house is tall and thin like a doll's house.
Pictures are filling in the walls,
but where the paint shows through in a chink
it is the authentic dull pink of oxblood and lime.

We take tea in the garden which is like a well
with its high walls, and deep shade and the underwater
grey-green of the thyme lawn; and sitting still like a still
ancient cloistered thing at the bottom of a well

she remembers (she must remember) a long trip
to the only part of Canada where it never snows,
weeks and weeks of sky and sea and sickness like snow-sickness.

Ever after a drawing-in, this square
of London sky, and the cypress leaning over.

Home County

Sparrows caught and hung in the thatch.
The South Downs hung over us.
In the neighbouring field, heifers wept for their calves.

A bluebell-wood harboured logs in the guise of crocodiles, foul
    mud that sucked in children's boots, and once free of the
        wood, where to go but the arid chalk heath winding
                unrelentingly on and up?

Pity the Romans their blue knees, their fluttering tunics, the flat,
                grey light.

A child's cradle in torn white brocade decorated the corner of the
                music room.
At Easter, the land was blessed. The vicar's name was Canon Dagger.
The young crops lay down and shivered in the east wind.

1976

We were not to mention the gold teeth
of Pedro, Nicaraguan prince and companion
of my godfather, Barry J. Gordon. All through lunch

the sunlight screeched off Pedro's canines
igniting the cutlery, the pine-cladding,
the tomato-red kitchen cabinets.

★

While my godfather swore blind the Staffordshire
pottery spaniel – seventeenth-century, royalist, red-haired –
belonged to him, *I want that fucking dog,*

my mother – regal, carolean – gave no ground,
Darling, you are dreadful. My father slunk about,
not up to the game, rightly punished.

★

By a curious and intricate choreography
my father made his way to my bedroom,
mapped out a constellation in phosphorescent stars,

retreated, reversing all the steps, leaning close in
to the dado, avoiding the creaky stair, was far away
when the lights went down, the applause began.

During the Blitz

Elizabeth stayed on in Greenwich, where her husband was employed in counter-espionage broadcasting for the BBC and, simultaneously, a cerebral and stimulating relationship with his secretary, Kathleen.

Elizabeth saw that the silver was polished, that no scraps were wasted, and barely flinched when a particularly heavy raid blew in the windows of the front elevation; shards of glass impaled themselves in the staircase and the panelling.

The children, now to be known only as major and minor, were removed to a progressive school in Kent where the playing fields, conveniently bordered on one side by a deep trench, lay directly beneath the flight-path of the incoming Luftwaffe.

In the dark, after lights-out, their father's words swam on through the ether, *Liebling, mein liebling, my pigeon, my dove.*

Zenith Automatic

In a small flat by the Thames, my father hoarded silver and china, pictures of his grandmother as a young woman with my profile, Staffordshire pottery figures, political cartoons of the eighteenth century, theatrical silhouettes, monogrammed napkin rings, a stone unicorn, glass-fronted bookcases, the family Bible, leather-bound books of naval history, a coat of arms, a writing-desk, a good paperknife, a Chinese vase.

In the last few days, these things took flight. Paintings, books and shepherdesses danced about his head. Nothing could be pinned down. It became important to fasten his father's watch directly onto my wrist from his own, which, according to the evidence of the perpetual mechanism, had already passed to an empty plain.

Thin

In an eyrie by the Thames, my mother is preparing for the summit.
What used to be a first-floor flat has grown higher and higher.
Even at base camp the air is thin. She is very high up.
She watches us all in her magnifying mirror, or doesn't bother.
Tea, cigarette, coffee, aspirin, cigarette, cigarette, wine, cigarette.
Cigarette, cigarette, cigarette, as the night draws in.
Days wax and wane. Soon it may be necessary to boil snow.
She is preparing her physical body for an extraordinary feat.
She is trying on her dresses. She is Wallis Simpson-thin.
Today, tomorrow or the next day, is the day she must be gone.

One Day a Herd of Wild Horses Came into the Garden and Looked at My Mother

Well, this is extraordinary, she is saying, *this is quite extraordinary*.

The horses stand on the grass and look at my mother.
My mother stands on the path and looks at the horses.
The horses nudge and shift; their manes tangle; their hooves are
                                                    caked in mud.

Not until the mare has turned her head, like a sail in the wind,
        away from the house and out toward the hills, and led each
                                straggling foal away, will my mother go
back into the house; close the door; pick up a book, a coffee, a
                                                    cigarette.

Estate

Cousin Gillian lives in a caravan by the shores of a lake in Canada, and in that caravan, so they say, she keeps Grandmother Elizabeth's long-case clock.

Some people do not think this an appropriate arrangement.
They think it heartless of her to keep so fine a piece
(school of Tompion) in such a dread abode.
Heartless and unthinking. How could she?
But I think it is a fine thing
which I would like to behold.

Is there a special orifice or protuberance of some kind
in the roof of the caravan through which or into which the clock
extends?
Does it lean jauntily within, and does this have any adverse effect
on the mechanism?
Do the bears and moose rouse to its bong bong bong?
How could such a wonder be, in any way, wrong?

It may be scooped out like a canoe
circling the lake at dawn and dusk; there would be room
for a packed lunch and the catch.
Might be a barricade, staunch
against the creatures of the night; it might be
out in all weathers; may serve as makeshift bench or table.
It might be firewood, a folly, or a totem pole –
it's possible, we just don't know.

Oh Gillian, cousin of my right hand! Cousin I have never met!
Let me, if some will not, bestow with happy heart
this ancient clock, to do with just as you see fit,
in praise of self-possession and the pioneering spirit.

Phyllis Pearl Dawn

Most loved, most beautiful, was my mother, Phyllis Pearl Dawn.
It was not wrong of her to think that all men would clamour at
                                                her door.
But this was easeful beauty of the dark almond eye, the perfect
                                                bone and brow.
If only she had learned envy and fight, struggle and plot,
like those who were not noble, but better equipped.

Cigarette Trees in Richmond Park

Where the boxcars all are empty
And the sun shines every day
And the birds and the bees
And the cigarette trees
The lemonade springs
Where the bluebird sings
In the Big Rock Candy Mountains
       Harry McClintock, 'Big Rock Candy Mountain'

No darling, I can't come with you, I'm going off through the park.
They say there's nothing whatsoever wrong with me it's all a big
                  mistake and there we are.
Such a beautiful evening – I've got my cab fare –
it's like the Serengeti sometimes, in high summer when the sun
                  lowers –
the deer and the yellow grass and a sort of thick haze like water
or old glass. And when Concorde goes over I love that, too, the
                  boom and then the arrow.
I think, actually, from now on, that is the way I should like to travel.

I've had enough of patience, and the jays in the garden at dawn
and the terrible sound of the foxes. Do you know the man who
                  feeds them,
and also – can you believe it – the rats? And an orphaned moorhen
tucked into his beard! But I'm bored of saving the scraps for him.
It's just that I've *done* it, do you know what I mean?

I've absolutely given up the Tube and those awful auditions.
It's so much more elegant to travel peacefully on the top deck
and have you noticed how empty the buses are, now, it's
                  wonderful?
There's always time for a coffee before you have to go in.
And, I meant to say, I've met that lovely man,
you know, the one with the big roll of notes, overalls,
the one who does something practical.
I can see a use for a man like that, and also he *is* kind.

The food's good, simple – soft-boiled eggs, stew, fruit straight
                                        from the trees,
that sort of thing; and always an open bottle of red in the evening
and at lunch a little pick-me-up. Do you know, I think this is the
                                        way to live.

And darling, time to read, time to sit and stare.
I *am* looking forward to you coming, darling,
when it suits. But don't worry about me. I'm going to sit here
like this and look at the water. I'll be absolutely fine.

Lilian's Letter

All the leaves are down on Ealing Common.
I love the spring.

Mozart is one of my favourite composers, & I enc. article re: him.
He died at 35. So v. young, poor man.

I've enjoyed book "The Horse Whisperer" but v. sad ending.
Author: Nicholas Evans.

I don't go out alone after dark.

I used to be a secretary and my favourite job was working for a
MARINE sales manager at ARBORITE dealing with shipping.
My boss, Mr Hill, had been a commander in the Royal Navy.
Sadly he died, due to a car crash. I had to visit his wife in their
lovely flat in Hampstead, & take his personal effects.

Please write, however briefly, as I enjoy letters.

★'Arborite' was a competitor to 'Formica', but they may have
closed now.
Our office was in W. Eal..

Words by Lilian Lewry

Naming the Baby

Call it Goathead, said the child
or *Lamppost, I don't care.*
And off she went with her imaginary friend, Cerys Butcher, a
                                    large, black hound.

Pantomime

I was one of those children who had to be coaxed.
The dancing-girl zeroed in, inviting, all teeth and eyes.
Yes, yes, bobbed the feather attached to her head.
No, no, no, no said my fingers, clutching the underside
of the red velvet seat where the nap was still good –
take the others, take the other children instead.
As they all clambered eagerly onto the stage I relaxed
my grip, put my theatrical career on ice.

Not Playing the Dane

He liked – or said he liked – best of all
a light cameo in the final act,
a decent armchair in the dressing-room,
not too much to learn, nothing *experimental*,
no doubling up, no hanging on for curtain call.

From the Pantechnicon

*Barry J. Gordon, a beautiful young boy with extraordinary golden hair,
first met Carl at a party that appeared to accommodate every anarchist,
communist, out-of-work actor, sailor, pimp and prostitute in town. From
the minute he set eyes on these unkempt and clay-covered people pouring
out of the back of a pantechnicon that accommodated Carl's wheelchair, he
was intrigued. Gordon became known as 'Carl's legs'.*

Framed photograph and newspaper cutting

William Beach
Champion Oarsman of the World

Photographed in Foley's Baths, Sydney, N.S.W.
September 25th 1888

Beach later claimed that his first earnings at 9 were for minding
cows on lush feed to stop them 'blowing', and that he then learnt
the trade of blacksmith. On 18 September 1886 he successfully
defended his title against Gaudar on the Thames; in this
exhausting race each rower in turn stopped and slumped in his
boat. Beach was then 5ft 9 1/2 ins. tall with a 42 ins. chest, 15
1/2 ins. biceps, 16 ins. calf and a weight of 170 lbs. Monuments
in his memory are at Cabarita Park, Sydney, and in Bill Beach
Park, Mullet Creek.

Playbill

Little Theatre Great Yarmouth
(Next to the Royal Aquarium)
DEATH GOES DANCING
A New and Exciting Comedy Thriller by Barry J Gordon
Front Stalls 6/-, Back Stalls 5/-, Balcony 4/-

Postcard from The Palace

Dear Mr Gordon,
    The Queen has commanded me to thank you for your card and for the record of her grandfather's speech at the opening of the Five Power Naval Conference on 21st January 1930. Her Majesty is delighted to accept this and greatly appreciated your kind thought in sending it to her. The Queen very much looks forward to listening to it.

Annotation to last will and testament applied by hand in green ink

    5 (g)   To P——K—— any other article of mine hereby not otherwise disposed of.

                                        – DELETE!

Letter from Murra Wurra

My Dear Barry,   17 ~~June~~ July 1958

I am afraid that this letter will greatly shock you. Heinz is dead. By his own hand last night. I can tell you very little except that he gassed himself. I do not know why as I have little contact with him as you know.
    I rang him Easter to tell him to write you. I wonder if he did? All very dreadful. I feel that it was inevitable as he had the

deathwish very strongly. I know you will feel dreadful about it and I am sorry I can not cushion the shock. I will write when I can tell you more. Of course there may be nothing to tell.

Love.

L [?] A [?]

Stapled, photocopied pages from Butler's Lives of the Saints

Saint Genesius the Comedian

In a comedy which was acted in the presence of the Emperor Diocletian in Rome, Genesius took it into his head to burlesque the ceremonies of Christian baptism. But here he was suddenly converted by a divine inspiration. The other players went through the whole ceremony of Baptism with him; but he in earnest answered the usual interrogatories, and on being baptized was clothed in a white garment.★

★Assuming this story to be true, the "baptism" administered would not be valid, for lack, on the part of the sacrilegious actor, of any intention even "to do what the Church does" when she baptizes. Genesius received the baptism, not of water, but of desire and blood.

Brass plaque removed from a dressing room at the Palace Theatre, Manchester

Barry J. Gordon
Singin' in the Rain

Poor quality photocopy of an entry in the register at Moonee Ponds, Victoria

I, Violet Lillian May Gordon, Spinster, of 24 Railway Place, Flemington do solemnly declare –

That the said John Gleason when a few months old was adopted by my mother Elizabeth Carmina Gordon in 1931 and was thereafter brought up by her and known as Barry John Gordon.

That I am the daughter of Elizabeth Carmina Gordon and the facts disposed to are within my own personal knowledge

and I take this solemn declaration conscientiously believing the same to be true and by virtue of the provisions of an Act of Parliament of Victoria rendering persons making a false declaration punishable for willful and corrupt perjury.

Manuscript in pencil and biro

DISTANCE
for Monté

We sigh with an ocean between –
Each wishing the other was near,
While Atlantic waves faded-green
Wash our thoughts 'cross the hemisphere …

~~But~~ As the moon ~~glides across~~ smiles in a single sky
And the one sun warms our skin
Each of us prays that soon we'll lie
Wrapped together – distance ~~the~~ our only sin.

London 1960

31

Form letter in plastic sleeve

To Whom it May Concern

I can confirm that the above patient is under our care at _____
_____ Hospital and is suffering _____ acute
_____ respectfully
request _____ bona fide _____ own personal
use _____ visiting your country.

Poem typescript

FOR LAST NIGHT

Here in a dream of the evening before
My unencumbered soul rests lightly
On the thought of your searching lips,
Your smooth torso wrapped round mine
And that warmth when I became part of you.
Often have I asked your eyes to smile –
And without beseeching (last night),
They engulfed me in their desire –
Invited me to lie with you,
Trusting, in your arms, and to kiss
Those textured limbs with loving grace.
We became as one and now I can hold
To my heart a dream long sought.

New York 1957

Articles torn from Encyclopaedia Britannica *and* Australasian
Pictorial Post

The Superb Lyrebird

When the male displays on top of large mounds, which he makes
at several places in the forest, he brings his tail forward so that the
white plumes form a canopy over his head and the lyre-like
feathers stand out to the side. In this position he sings, while
prancing in rhythm, far-carrying melodious notes interspersed
with perfect mimicry of other creatures and even of mechanical
sounds.

For the purposes of mating the female makes her selection
according to the male's beauty and skill in dancing.

★

He is a shy animal keeping mainly to the interior of the forest
rarely flying except to launch himself into the low branches of
trees with a heavy, slow wingbeat. If disturbed he will scuttle and
dodge along the the forest floor. He is, however, a survivor, and
many a person sheltering in a creek from a forest fire has
discovered, when the danger had passed, that he had been sharing
his sanctuary, and his blanket, with one of these remarkable
creatures.

The larynx of the superb lyrebird is bifurcated so that it may
sing simultaneously the call of two kookaburras in 'conversation',
or the entwined melodies of two distinct movements for the flute,
or the chainsaw and mechanical hammer in perfect rapport.

*Score, lyrics and Library of Congress Certificate of Copyright for a
Foreign Musical Composition*

Itchy Feet Blues

I got the itchy feet blues
I wanna be someplace else
I got the itchy feet blues

I wanna be movin'
I gotta be with my man [gal] – or else
I'll keep on moonin'
I wanna see those stars
from the other side
Jupiter holdin'
hands with Mars
That's why
I got the itchy feet blues
Got the itchy feet blues

II

The Republic of the Husband

The Effect of Spaceflight on the Female Body

Hear my song, Val – en – tee – hee – na.
Hear my song, in my gondola.
I am singing.
I am Seagull.
I can see fires burning in South America, and cities at night.
The light of the moon on the dark side of the earth is very
beautiful.
I have tried but failed to observe the solar corona.
I am not afraid to fall to earth.
My capsule is very small.
I had excellent communications with Yastreb on the first orbit,
but these have faded and it is no longer possible to speak
directly.

I am homesick for the sound of rain.

Dolls in National Dress

Not only am I
(Belgium)
the lady making lace with real turning bobbins

I am also
(Canada)
the Eskimo family

daddy mummy baby in papoose
one two three heads in circles of fur
and

(España)
flounces of scarlet and black.

Seventeen Poems About Adultery

Seventeen poems about adultery
in one slim volume
is too many
even if they have a historical element
or are veiled.

Furthermore,
the poet's wife is apologising for her lack of verbal craft
and here we all are, eating her canapés
in bad clothes, flitting our eyes about, taking notes.

Dear lady, my heart goes out to you.
Go off with your horse on the blasted heath.
Poetry is not verse-making.

No Sex, Again

All my poems are evasions.
Never, never shall I speak of that ordinary, terrible subject,
the *one* subject, you might have thought.

English, to the cold, cold, marrow of my bones.
No sex. Like the play my father did, on and off, for years
and always in the reps – 'What's Robert doing now?'
'*No Sex…*, darling, *again*!'

There's something about a woman and something about a poem:
Dickinson's white skirts, her intimate knowledge of botany, even
                              of the orchid and the stinking hellebore;
Rossetti high and dry and burning; the three-cornered, fuck-off
                              hat of Marianne Moore;
Elizabeth's render of, not ice, but salt, and a sheathed knife;
that vicious Mary Sidney scourging and pointing the finger.

The Hula-hula Girl and the Reeds at the Water's Edge

She is dancing in circles all around you
touching not a hair of your head.

She is balancing a basket of wax fruit
like a hat or an offering.

Someone is wearing a grass skirt. *Hush hush*
say the reeds at the water's edge.

Electricity

You are electric your hair stands on end.
Your pointy fingers pulse volts and terrific blue lightning.

You are quick as a shock and you think nothing of lighting up the
grid.
If you were a sort of man-god you'd be like those pylons striding
over the land.

What I am saying is I find you electrifying.
You fire on all circuits. I am more of a slow glow,

a bit stolid if you want to know.
It *could* work.

Falling

I had been falling a long time,
but the journey was pleasant enough,
and interesting even when difficult.
At night we skirted the Fortunate Isles,
The Bay of Plenty, but I didn't know it,
for we travelled without map or sextant,
proving en route and quite fortuitously
a number of universal laws.

Arrived thirsty and lean, touching down,
inexplicably, in the pure dead
centre of a dry land on red dust
where a great rock stood, obdurate,
foolish and familiar, to the open sky;
and from the helm of the rock nothing,
but lesser monoliths and a line
of pilgrims in summer clothes who had paid
good money to witness this strange thing
in the desert, undiminished and enduring.

The Terrible Poem

I want to write a poem that will slay you.
I want to knock you off your feet.
I want to send you stumbling and gasping and clutching your heart.
I want you to have to make excuses and to break out in a cold sweat.
My God, I want you to ask, *is this — it?*

The Vulgar Muse

You have come out of the bitter lake.
You have come sliding towards me with set jaw.
You have rolled in with the fog and the drear,
and pressed me to your flaccid breast.
Sparks fly from your dress.
Your hair is like the warrior's helmet.
Your skin is white as the corpse, and your hair black.
You have stopped my nostrils with your scent
and my throat with your powder.
You have dressed me in your heavy red with tissues in the pocket.
You have taken from me the flagon and the bread
and fed me ashes and salt.
You have taken from me my soft skin, my hope
and all my treasures, my Bible and the carpet from my feet,
and nothing, nothing have you given me.

Arthur's Pictures

i

The foolish lion is chasing the naked woman.
The pedals of the piano loll like swollen tongues;
the strings are spent.
I do not like the chances of her naked rump.

ii

Nebuchadnezzar claws the ground like the beast he is.
Something evil and pitiable is forming in the yellow light.

iii

The woman is all light –
her hair is golden light,
and her white clothes, diaphanous light,
and everything between us is light;
her touch upon me is light, and light
go her feet in their white slippers.
Her laughter's nothing but intensities of light.

The Girl in the Tree

The girl in the tree
is not a good girl.

She is of the family of tree,
slender in wrinkled tights and a summer dress.
Her hair is brown and her eyes are black as anything.

She is dangled precariously,
but not really,
a foot or less from the grasp of her father who stands below
with palms upturned and a tense neck.
The girl in the tree is crying; she won't come down
or let herself be saved.

We are all looking at the girl in the tree.

She is of the tribe of the elf and her eyes are black.
She turns her back and points her pointy toes
and gives a wobble.
Her arms are slender as a young branch of this small tree.

Her mother is blonde and the baby is blonde
and the mother is oh so easy with all the
baby chemicals and the circularity of the baby
who really is enjoying this unexpected late summer sun
and does not know about the loftiness of trees and a black look.

Virginia Creeper Very High Up in the Yard

These branches severed twenty feet above the ground
cling on in fanned shapes of stuccoed trees.
These are the undergarments, the fixings unearthed.

We've lived in the dark, feeling our way, unseeing for years
the tracery of roots that makes our chamber roof,
the skeleton of a leaf that covers us, delta

of vein and capillary opening out
into the fingers of an open hand.
Nothing is hidden.

Lessons

Just because a man shows you a white stag on a brown hill, it
                                    doesn't mean he's got soul.

Just because he walks you down the Corpse Road, it doesn't
                                    mean he's got soul.

Just because he knows this black lake is the deepest lake in
                                    England, doesn't mean

Just because the clock-maker and the coffin-maker dance to the
                                    same tune

Just because he's charmless it doesn't mean he's true.

The Mighty Gyrfalcon and the Lowly Pigeon

Dad saw a gyrfalcon destroying a pigeon in Jill's garden.
It escaped from a bird place; we heard it on the radio.

[pause]

It was eating the pigeon.

Bless you, my sweet child, bearer of sweet news.

None of These Things is Completely White

An arctic hare,
a gyrfalcon,
that old stag on the hill.

The falcon's pantaloons and the
pigeon's down, lifting and lifting
like summer clouds.

The Republic of the Husband

All the people have run mad.
They have left the open squares, the wide boulevards.
It is the mistral coming in and in from the sea, always
and forever without remission.
Only the rubber trees bend in the avenue.

In one of these charming buildings, the pen
of a general is scratching something elaborate
and carefully worded; it is a treaty or an abdication,
he forgets which. Twice a day his boots sound
in the portico. The marble is spotless.

The Husband Behind the Wall

The husband behind the wall is listening closely to every word.
He is trying to keep us all on the straight and narrow.
He is an upright citizen of some republic or other.

Much as he would like to believe I did not exist,
I make it very difficult for him.
He catches every lift of my voice; it is seeping through,
spoiling the plasterwork like a violent mosaic.
I think I will save him some egg boxes and some glue and a small
                      spatula and he can make arrangements,
because, after all, the wall itself has become a bone of contention,
its leanings and liltings, its peelings and parings.
But it is no good pretending he is not mine,

that I am not his.
I have stationed him there, a sad policeman who has heard too much.
One of these days he will have a mind to give up on me entirely
                      and then where shall we be.

Kind

This is a lovely sadness.
It is grey-blue and extremely elegant.
A beautiful clever woman
is drinking alone in a bar
or on her own in her own flat
contemplating something final,
listening to the birds.

Odds and ends of days,
crosswords and patience
at a kitchen table,
a glass of wine at dusk
and then the long pull
through the long hours
and the short hours,
a sick, orange glow over London
and the planes come in low
all night, all day.

All those beautiful clever women
of a certain age, a certain Age,
in New York, Paris, London
and, yes, even in the provinces.
Come on over, they seem to be saying,
we're having a ball. Think of the jokes,
think of the conversation.

Benediction

I can't love you, Carruthers,
but I am sending the birds to sing through your head into the
empty spaces.

III

Land- and Seascapes

Signal Flags

When I think of all the great tall ships –
signals ripping through a red sky –
the tiny men on board
and all those lives ended
and hard lives, and short,
and some no more than boys,
I am moved nonetheless by the beautiful words.

How did the land bear when last seen?
Indicate the bearing of the light.

I am unmanageable.

and
What were your last observations for time?
We are in danger of parting.

And Iago's stage whisper:
Keep a good look out as it is reported that enemy's war vessels are going
about disguised as merchantmen.

The ropes fraying and the flags disordered and sodden and the
slow hoist.

Have you a surgeon?

And this:
Being in distress, and obliged to part company on that account, when the
state of the weather will not admit of acquainting the commander of the
convoy of the occasion thereof.

Finding America

In deep midwinter once I saw
where tyrant tide with hungry maw
tore wave and scree together from the shore,
all prone, and round about, and here and there,
a submerged forest in the open air.

The burl I held was like a heel
kept from fire but not from flood;
something more than ice and wind
shook me, chilled me to the bone –

the wreckage of a ship unbuilt
the timbers scattered fore and aft,
and mighty oaks in sapless disarray revealed
for our instruction, yearly, in the bitter cold.

The Random Nature of God

might be in these piebald horses
rampant under a full moon in an ancient field in midwinter.
All I can tell you is this: there was power, kindliness and great
                                                    danger
and many things happened that could not be.

I think particularly of hooves on an old stone bridge –
narrow low and smooth over bog and rivulet – the horses could
                                                    not cross,
but did, approaching side on, each one appearing, like a pole-
                    vaulter or an articulated truck, to overshoot,
in order to achieve the tricky move;
the scrape and slide of iron on rock and the calling
for kin and comrade, the falling
into rhythm, the panic at separation, the trampled gates and
                                                    fences;
an advance-guard sortie up the lane towards the main road and
                                        certain carnage;

my own voice screaming *Chip, Chip, Chip,*
into the night like a demented bird
and pulling the little dog
from under the great clattering hooves unharmed;
the horse-man on the telephone who spoke no word of English
I could understand but *no problem* and *top field, top field.*
I see, I said, politely, and *thank you,* and *goodbye,*
knowing my situation at once for what it was,
the rules, conventions, tropes as in a dream
of convoluted plots, the saviour telephone that melts and slides,
escaping legs that will not turn;

the way that progress happens: as one horse breached the ditch
that leap made possible the feat for many others coming after
and those that failed found other routes as yet unthought-of
until the drive, garden, fields, sheds, barns,
all were host to the great mild panicking beasts.

And the thing I must set down because it is
the notion I can't give up, that something in me,
in us, drew on the horses. Two years
of peaceful untroubled grazing ended
on our one night alone in that place,
the first breach the field by the house where jaws
and teeth and a kind of hunger led the way
to what seemed richer grass on our side of the trench.

If it's a visitation and a blessing it's also a responsibility –
boundlessness seeks its own limits,
immoderation calls for keeping house and making good
and the re-introduction, in daylight, of strong fences.

And something else to keep in mind –
that last view of the horses, in sunlight,
stepping easily though the long grass
to the far gate and safe pasture,
remote and almost out of sight. Consider
there's as much in that practised, familiar retreat
as in all the night's Sturm und Drang.

Harvest Hare

On the occasion of a reading by Paul Muldoon at the University of Exeter,
26 October 2011

Paul Muldoon saw a hare at Exeter University.
Where is the hare at Exeter University Paul Muldoon saw?

It has gone off into the undergrowth, such as it is,
into the tall grass by the artificial lake,

into the deeper dark beneath the specimen trees.
They are all electric and needling this October sky.

December Hare

There is the haze.
The haze hangs over a far field.

But where is the hare?
The hare is nowhere.

These are all the places where
the hare is not:
He is not on the ice or under the oak.
He is not at the trough with the sheep.
He is not in the ploughed
or in the flooded field.
He knows not swan
or pheasant, rook or wren.

But, hare, you have not been
forgotten. Everywhere I look,
I see a clearing or a nook
where the hare is not.
He is not that piece of wood,
that root on a bank.
No, it is only a root,
it is only a piece of wood.
He is not that rock by the stream.

Though the hare
is nowhere to be seen
I feel his gaze. The low sky
is like a pelt, the sun
one cold eye.

What if the hare
should suddenly appear
here on this verge
to leap and gambol
right across your field

of vision; or two hares
boxing, one in his winter coat;
or a whole family, a drove
in procession, dancing
and performing tricks
and wearing hats, what then?

I would say, *hare is there.*

February Hare

This is the time and the place before the hare
where such an animal was unthought.

It's snow-melt that's made the river red
and in the field a line of liquid green
is showing where the flood has been.

But of the hare, not a trace of a trace of a trace.
Call for him, he will not come,
in form or out of it, hare is all undone.

The Sacred and the Drear

What wise spirits dance in the wake of radiator man?
Or the twitcher with his expensive binoculars
hoping for that precious glimpse?
He, too, awaits the descent of a creature from the upper regions.

The circulation of the central heating is something like
the pull of tide and moon, and the cycle of the seasons –
laws physical and universal. Do not dismiss him.
Nor the woman who excels at the buffet
or the dinner party. We are all God's creatures.

It is good to know the soundness of the heavens above us
and of the earth beneath our feet,
and it is good to know the joists run east to west,
not north to south, that the A1 is the road less travelled
at this hour and on a bank holiday in May,
and the name of the last four landlords of the Three Feathers in
                                                    Godalming,
for that is the name of God's pantler, his hostelry man.
Each in his own way and by his own nature.

The Biochemistry of Beasts

Nails, and in the scales
and paws of reptiles,
their shells, and in the feathers,
beaks and claws of birds,
the quills of porcupine, the plates
of filter-feeding whales,
protective armour and the bills
of dinosaurs, the silk
of pupae and the fibres
of a web, the casing
of an egg, the hornet's nest.
The horse's hoof, and in the hair
of wolf, the lamb's fleece,
the lion's mane, the horn
of buffalo and unicorn.

The Angel of Necessity

Angel of Necessity, you are my favourite angel;
you flinch not and are always prepared.
I see you now, coming over the mountain,
with your sandals and your possibles bag
of worked leather.

You are something like the muse –
merciless and love-created.

Do not think only of hardship and burden;
think also of the many lovely things that must and shall be –

the cabin she has built,
the fish in the creek,
the little alpine flowers blossoming under her heel
where extremity binds the roots
and makes piercing the bluebell's blue.

Idyll

for Mike and Alison Harvey

Two frogs and a toad,
each scarcely bigger
than a money spider,
have come into the house
in the furl of a leaf,
in the cluster of small
green hearts which spills in
under the back door,
making, of the leaking
roof and the creeping
damp, a garden.

Making Dens

If I must make a small place to crawl inside of
and I think I must – it is the work of all our days –
I hope it will be well-made and imperfect
so that when the job is done and I am safe inside,
I may see, through a flaw in the ceiling, sky
and at the makeshift door, a blade or two of grass.

Starlings

Leafless trees are flourishing their fingertips
    up high like children being trees in P.E.
        in the 1970s, in pants and vest,
            and finding it not unfreeing.

Branches ring with birdsong, but the birds are
    unbelievably still, still as the breathing
        girls in arabesque at the Moulin Rouge, and
            everything is broadcast backwards

all at once, at the wrong speed, on a machine
    that whirs and clicks: a few bars of an old tune
        sung just off-key, the falcon's cry, the owl's screech.
        Basic research, says the starling,

I have a question. Listen up, professor.
    Is this your moment of wonderful invention?
        Eddison? Browning? Mozart knew a piss-
            artist when he saw one – bird-brain,

amigo, little trickster; no-one but you
    would bastardise my melody. That's genius
        right there. In Piccadilly, a fountain mouths
        'The Lake Isle of Innisfree' and

William Yeats is not so very far from home.
    Nor are we ever, nor lost, nor out of step;
        what comes back late comes back with a vengeance. *Mort*
      imer, and again, *Mortimer*.

Mind in his Cage

Poor little mind
shaking his bars,
so little, so feeble.

He has bound his tears into rope
and the rope is a cage,
his hands blistered,
his throat raw,

far above the flowers,
the seep of wet soil,
the smell of earth.

No vapours reach him
and his ears are deaf
to the spheres, deaf
to the birds.

Flood

Water everywhere. Rivers brim and flood.
The fields *are* rivers. I'm trying to tell you what it is like here.
The colours are black, green and silver: water, grass and swan.
It is always evening and we are always retreating from the scene
or the scene retreating from us. It is true to say that when I
see this I see it through your eyes.

Signal Flags (Without You It's Chaos)

In faded Kodachrome you cycle the towpath,
juggling stopwatch, megaphone, spectacles, paunch,
booming plummy instructions to a boatful of young historians.
Without you it's chaos.

Those Edwardian vowels carry over the river.
I catch your drift, imagine an encounter
tall ship to tall ship in open water.

No good telling me (white over blue)
Engage the enemy more closely
or even (scarlet) *Give wine to the rowers*
for *I'm astray, I cannot tow you.*

On one of these dark days, hugging my misery,
I can lay hands on nothing but yellow
for *Quarantine*, black for *Shipwreck*. Our one hope?

Evening, and a sunset in the French style
(dawn, fawn and isabelle, moiré, dead-leaf,
blue Turkish, carmine, flax-grey, purple).

Youth, thou art banish-ed.
You were not all they promis-ed.
Sweet, galling, dimpled, over-fed –
I am glad that you have fled.

Notes

'Lilian's Letter'
Lilian Lewry lives in Ealing where she paints, crafts and writes.

'From the Pantechnicon'
The epigraph is adapted from Darleen Bungey, *Arthur Boyd: A Life* (2007), p. 185.

'The Effect of Spaceflight on the Female Body'
When Valentina Tereshkova became the first woman in space, her mission objective was the collection of data on the response of the female body to spaceflight. The poem uses and adapts translations of some of Tereshkova's own words recorded in-flight and in subsequent interviews.

'No Sex, Again'
No Sex Please, We're British is a farce by Alistair Foot and Anthony Marriott that played to packed houses in the 1970s and 80s.

'Arthur's Pictures'
The title refers to the Australian painter Arthur Boyd (1920–99).